D0773347

SEEDS OF FAITH

Peace

SEEDS OF FAITH

Peace

Words of Faith from
NORMAN VINCENT PEALE

Ideals Publications · Nashville, Tennessee

ISBN 0-8249-4647-2

Published by Ideals Publications, a division of Guideposts
535 Metroplex Drive, Suite 250, Nashville, Tennessee 37211
www.idealsbooks.com

Editor, Peggy Schaefer
Designer, Marisa Calvin
Cover photograph: David Cook/www.blueshiftstudios.co.uk/Alamy

Printed and bound in Mexico by RR Donnelley
10 9 8 7 6 5 4 3 2 1

ACKNOWLEDGMENTS
All Scripture quotations are taken from The King James Version of the Bible.

Photography credits: Page 3, David Cook/www.blueshiftstudios.co.uk/ Alamy; page 5, J. Schwanke/Alamy; page 8, age fotostock/SuperStock; page 10, Ken Fowler/Alamy; page 15, age fotostock/SuperStock; page 27, Mark Cassino/SuperStock; page 32, joSon/SuperStock; page 39, Jeff Compasso/Alamy.

Take plenty of time to contemplate
the vast peace of God;
it is so deep and full and kindly
that we cannot comprehend it.
—Norman Vincent Peale

FOREWORD

Throughout his long career, my father, Norman Vincent Peale, valued no message more than that of the importance of faith in each of our lives. In fact, before the title was finalized, *The Power of Positive Thinking* was called *The Power of Faith*. It was that important to him.

Growing up in the Midwest at the beginning of the twentieth century, Dad learned about faith at his parents' knees and in the pews of small-town churches. Faith in God, country, and fellow man, and the saving message of Jesus Christ filled his youthful days. He learned oratorical skills by listening to the great preachers of the day,

who went from town to town, bringing countless people to faith. He became filled with faith messages, and they never left him.

When the personal call came for him to enter the ministry, Dad was well equipped with deep faith, a gift for communicating, and a love of people. His writings were full of anecdotes of the faith journeys of countless people he met along the way. By their examples, he was able to lead others to a life of faith. His was a great calling, and I think we can all agree that he succeeded.

As you read, I hope you enjoy the messages in this book and that it brings deeper faith into your life.

—*Elizabeth Peale Allen*

And the peace of God, which passeth all understanding, shall keep your hearts and minds through Christ Jesus. —PHILIPPIANS 4:7

The ability to live peacefully, quietly, and serenely with oneself is surely one of the greatest skills available to human beings. It is inside the human being that the storms and the tempests surge. It is inside the mind that pain and conflict occur.

Having peace of mind does not mean that

everything becomes easy and light. We live in a world of tumult, stress, trouble, and conflict. But we are better able to handle these when we are inwardly quict and controlled. The text from Isaiah 26:3 suggests the way in which this is done: "Thou wilt keep him in perfect peace, whose mind is stayed on thee." This means, of course, that if you get your mind off your conflicts and onto God, really trusting Him, you will master the skill of living at peace with yourself. What we become inwardly depends on what we think inwardly. If you have unpeaceful thoughts, you are not going to be peaceful. If you learn to think calmly and confidently, you become calm and confident. So you must learn to discipline and control your thinking.

Do you want to live with peace and quiet in a noisy world? The first thing to do is to fill your mind with thoughts of peace. A second thing is to not take yourself too seriously. By taking yourself too seriously, you can ultimately get to the point where you almost imagine that all civilization stands or falls on what you do. The remedy, as I see it, and as I think we are taught, is to love God, love people, serve the Lord, do the best you can—and then, "having done all," as Saint Paul says, "stand" (Ephesians 6:13).

And I have to add one more thing. You can work hard at thinking the right kind of thoughts and you can try to get yourself in proper perspective, but you will never do either unless you are under the right kind of control. And the only control that will guarantee an individual's ability to live at peace with himself is, in my humble judgment, to live with Jesus. If a person has Jesus deep in his mind and really has in him that "mind . . . which was also in Christ Jesus" (Philippians 2:5), then he thinks the kind of thoughts that Christ thought. If he has Jesus in his heart, then he is serene and confident, knowing that no matter what comes in the way of opposition, difficulty, pain, sorrow, or death, Jesus is with him—the everlasting Friend. Jesus Christ has a strange and mystic influence on human beings: the peace of God is found through Jesus Christ our Lord.

One thing about peace is certain: you will never get it by struggling for it. The more you struggle for peace of mind, the less likely you will ever get it. Nor will you ever find it by searching

Thou wilt keep him in perfect peace, whose mind is stayed on thee.

ISAIAH 26:3

for it. In fact, you will never get it by pursuing it at all. You will get it by being receptive. Jesus Christ said: "Peace I give unto you." That is very significant. It is a gift—not a struggle. "Peace I give unto you: not as the world giveth, give I unto you. Let not your heart be troubled, neither let it be afraid" (John 14:27).

Peace of mind is within your reach; you must reach out for it to receive it. If I want to give you something, I hold out my hand with the gift. But you cannot receive this gift unless you reach out and take it. It is just that simple. Jesus offers peace—you can have it if you take it. You can

have it right now if you take it. But if you think you have to struggle and engage in strategy and search and keep after it, then it will always elude you. Peace of mind is a gift. You can have it by reaching for it.

One of the things that holds us back from peace of mind is the undue emphasis on materialistic values that we have. More recent generations have come to lay great importance on certain things in which peace of mind is not inherent. As the faith in spiritual things has declined, we have seized upon a piteous faith in material things. We feel that if we can just accumulate so

much, have so many things, develop a high degree of comfort and prosperity, we will be secure and have peace and serenity.

Now, I realize that having enough money in the bank to pay your bills is a good thing. I believe that a person should accumulate whatever material goods are consistent with his best life. And I see no inconsistency in solid free enterprise, provided we also have solid spiritual thinking and sharing. But you have got to keep it in balance.

For example, I was in Los Angeles and Beverly Hills once when they had a terrible fire up in Topanga Canyon in the Bel Air district. Five hundred homes were destroyed. This area is occupied, for the most part, by people who have very beautiful homes. I was close enough to smell the fire and to see the flames. It was an awesome sight.

Well, I felt very sorry for those people. Some of them had lost everything. I called up one woman I knew whose home was in the line of the fire. "How is the situation out there?" I asked.

"Oh, Norman," she said, "I don't know what I am going to do. This fire is getting nearer every day. Last night I cried myself to sleep. What if I should lose my house?"

"Well, Mary," I said, "if you lose that house,

A harvest of
peace is produced
from a seed of
contentment.

AUTHOR
UNKNOWN

you can always get another." That was exactly the wrong thing to say to her.

"I am surprised that you have no more sympathy for me than that," she replied sharply. "Don't you know that everything I value in life is in this house? This is my nest. If I lose this house, I have lost everything." Well, that is pretty grim—when you have lost everything if you lose your house.

I called up another friend of mine, whose home was high on a hill in Topanga Canyon, a beautiful house. I have been in it. It was burned to the ground within an hour—everything in it was destroyed. So I called him up and said, "I am sorry you lost your house."

Do you know what he said? "Now listen, Norman, don't you worry about me. Jane and the kids are safe and our family is together. The house was only material goods. We struggled for it and we built it and we enjoyed it, but we are together and we will build another house. Don't worry about me. This is just one of those little roadblocks on the way of life. If I really get into spiritual trouble, then I'll want you to come around sympathizing with me." Now there's a great man, with peace of mind and a sense of values.

Is it possible to have peace of mind with conditions in the world as they are? Of course it is. And without inner peace, a person will not have much happiness or good health and will not be able to contribute much to improve world conditions.

Many people think that the time they live in is the most troubled in all of human history. Some even feel that in the face of present-day conditions, it isn't proper to have peace of mind. I have read the history books, and I cannot put my finger on any period when things were perfect. To have peace of mind at all, we must learn to have it now, right where we are.

Jesus said, "Peace I give unto you: not as the world giveth, give I unto you. Let not your heart be troubled, neither let it be afraid" (John 14:27). So I speak in defense of peace of mind.

How, then, does one develop peace of mind? I'll give you one important part of the answer. You do it by emptying your mind of things contrary to peace of mind: hate, selfishness, prejudice, smugness, impurity, fear, anxiety. One of the healthiest processes known to man is a catharsis of the mind, in which you empty from your system those things which destroy peace of mind.

The average person, before retiring at night, usually empties his or her pockets onto the dresser or desk. Personally, I rather enjoy standing over a wastepaper basket during this process to see how many things I can throw away: notes, memos, scraps of paper, completed self-directions, even knickknacks that I have picked up. With relief, I deposit all items possible in the wastepaper basket.

It occurred to me one night that I ought to empty my mind as I empty my pockets. During the day we pick up many mental odds and ends: a little worry, a little resentment, a few annoyances, some irritations, perhaps even some guilt reactions. Every night these should be drained off; for, unless eliminated, they accumulate.

And how do you drain the thoughts? I suggest that you think of your mind as a sink with a stopper in the bottom. Mentally remove the stopper and imaginatively "see" the mass of soiled material disappear down the drain. Then mentally replace the stopper and fill the mind with clean, wholesome, spiritual thoughts.

You must be careful in performing this

And let the peace of God rule in your hearts . . . and be ye thankful.

COLOSSIANS 3:15

process not to take a thought back. When you have drained it out, conceive of it as gone. If your mind attempts to reach out for the old thought, stop it by saying, "That thought is gone forever, removed by God's grace, and I will not take it back."

One night, I came home to find my wife experimenting with some new accessories for her vacuum cleaner. She showed me a long-arm attachment with which dust could be sucked out of hidden corners. While I was admiring this mechanical gadget, it occurred to me that a similar spiritual mechanism could be employed to draw "dust" out of our thoughts.

So I developed for myself a vacuum-cleaner prayer: "Dear Lord, by the power of Thy Spirit, draw now from the unseen crannies and crevices of my soul the dust of the world that has settled there."

Try this. The resulting sense of cleanness will add to your inner peace.

Another method is to figuratively and imaginatively reach into your mind, as though you could put your fingers into your brain and lift out unhappy thoughts one by one. As you imagine yourself doing this, affirm: "I am now taking out and throwing away that fear, that prejudice, that resentment, that impure recollection." Then, when the mind is thus emptied, affirm: "I am now putting into my mind the pure thoughts of Christ. I am asserting the love of God, the goodness of our Lord."

Before you have ever completed this process, the kindly Heavenly Father, who is pleased when His children thus deal with themselves, will have enfolded you in His kindly peace.

We have come to the time when we—both ministers of the Gospel and physicians of the mind and body—realize that peace of mind is absolutely necessary to physical well-being and that physical well-being is not possible when the mind is filled with dark, unreasonable thoughts.

The secret to change lies in your thoughts and mental attitude. If you want to live at peace with yourself, you must integrate thoughts of peace, beauty, and goodness. And like everything else, this is a disciplinary process that requires practice. I have a little trick that I use when I begin to get edgy. I call it "remembered peacefulness."

One time, in the midst of activities which I had

Do not be
afraid of tomorrow,
for God is
already there.
AUTHOR
UNKNOWN

foolishly allowed to become hectic, I went to Atlantic City. From my window I could look out directly upon the sea as it washed gently on soft shores of sand. It was very quieting to behold this scene. The day was overcast with drifting fog and clouds. Imperturbably the sea rolled shoreward with its deep-throated roar and ceaseless but perfect rhythm. Clean spume flew from its wave crests. Over the beach, and climbing high against the sky before sliding down the wind with ineffable grace, sea gulls soared and dived.

Everything in the scene was graceful, beautiful, and conducive to serenity. Its benign peacefulness laid a healing, quieting touch upon me. I closed my eyes and discovered that I could still visualize the scene just as I had beheld it. There it was, as clear as when actually viewed by the eye. It occurred to me that the reason I could "see it" with my eyes closed was because my memory had absorbed it and was able to reproduce it in detail.

Why, then, I reasoned, could I not live again and again in this scene of quiet beauty, even though bodily absent from the place?

So I began the practice of deliberately visualizing quiet scenes of beauty in which I had once actually lived.

Sometimes, in the midst of active work, I

have found it beneficial to stop for a minute or two and bring up out of memory's storehouse scenes that had impressed me by their beauty—and to experience once again their remarkable power to quiet, soothe, and relax.

For example, I have found that when sleep comes with difficulty, I can actually induce slumber by visualizing scenes of quietness and peace. Lying in a relaxed manner in my bed, I practice going back as far as I can remember and recollecting one by one the truly peaceful experiences of my life, such as the time I gazed upon Mount Blanc when the vast mountain was bathed in moonlight. Or the radiant, sun-kissed morning when our great white ship dropped anchor in the blue waters off Waikiki Beach in Hawaii. Or that mystic evening when I first watched the purple shadows fill the Grand Canyon to overflowing with a hush. Or watching the sunlight sift through ancient maple trees onto the green lawn on a summer afternoon at my farm home. As I traverse these marvelous scenes of beauty and peace through the power of memory to recreate them, God's quietness overcomes me, and I drift into a sound and untroubled sleep.

So, now and then, let go of your cares and the

problems of the day, and wander in memory among the most beautiful places you have ever lived. Repeat out loud peaceful words. Words have profound suggestive power, and there is healing in the very saying of them. Use a word such as "serenity." Picture serenity as you say it. Repeat it slowly and in the mood of which the word is a symbol. This will quiet you, and as you yield yourself to the benign power of quiet visualization, you will find rest and relaxation.

It is also helpful to use lines from poetry or passages from the Scriptures. A man of my acquaintance who has achieved a remarkable peace of mind has the habit of writing on cards unusual quotations expressing peacefulness. He carries one of the cards in his wallet at all times, referring to it frequently until each quotation is committed to memory. He says that each such idea dropped into the subconscious "lubricates" his mind with peace. One of the quotations he used is from a sixteenth-century mystic: "Let nothing disturb you. Let nothing frighten you. Everything passes away except God. God alone is sufficient."

If you have never tried dropping Bible passages into your tired or agitated mind, I cannot urge you too strongly to experiment with the

He leadeth me
beside the still waters.
He restoreth my soul.

PSALM 23:2-3

process at once. Cares, worries, decisions, and exasperations, multiplied during the day, bring the mind to the point where it wants to escape. So the mind needs to be refreshed, and this is accomplished by lifting consciousness to a higher level.

To a certain extent, beautiful music, a quick change of scenery, a joke, or a diverting experience will accomplish this momentarily. But the form of thought diversion that reaches the deeper levels of consciousness most effectively is a Bible verse. Why? Perhaps because it comes from the most trusted Book. It is basic truth. It is God's Word. It contains the healing power of Christ's spirit.

Probably what happens is that a Bible verse brings so much faith into your mind that it drives off weariness, for weariness is but another form of negativism.

Repeat the chosen verses aloud slowly. Saying the words out loud impresses them more deeply upon your consciousness by adding hearing to sight. When said slowly, the full melody of the text is brought out. Moreover, each word in a Bible passage has significance, and a slow vocalization tends to emphasize the full meaning of each separate, precious word and syllable. It is also valuable and important to commit these passages to memory

and to articulate them at intervals during the day, especially when you may tend to feel a bit down. Search the Scriptures to discover for yourself passages that seem especially meaningful to you.

There are other practical ways by which you can develop serenity and quiet attitudes. One way is through your conversation. When the conversation in a group takes a trend that is upsetting, try injecting peaceful ideas into the talk. To have peace of mind, fill your personal and group conversations with positive, happy, optimistic, satisfying expressions.

Another effective technique in developing a

peaceful mind is the daily practice of silence. Insist upon not less than a quarter of an hour of absolute quiet every twenty-four hours. Go alone into the quietest place available to you, and sit or lie down for fifteen minutes and practice the art of silence. Do not write or read. Think as little as possible. Throw your mind into neutral. Conceive of your mind as the surface of a body of water and see how nearly quiet you can make it, so that there is not a ripple. When you have attained a tranquil state, listen for the deeper sounds of harmony and beauty and God that are to be found in the essence of silence.

First keep the peace
within yourself, then
you can also bring
peace to others.
THOMAS À KEMPIS

Saturate your thoughts with peaceful experiences, peaceful words and ideas, and ultimately you will have a storehouse of peace-producing experiences to which you may turn for refreshment and renewal of your spirit. It will be a vast source of power.

Every human being wants inner peace. And everyone can have it—deep, unshakable inner peace. You can have the inner peace you've always wanted through the gift to you and me of

Jesus Christ. “Peace I leave with you, my peace I give unto you: not as the world giveth, give I unto you. Let not your heart be troubled, neither let it be afraid” (John 14:27). Surely no words more beautiful than these were ever uttered. And in these marvelous sentences is one explanation of the profound hold of Jesus Christ upon the human heart.

The peace that comes through Jesus Christ—the only kind worth having—is the very source of the power we need for meeting the responsibilities in our lives and meeting them effectively. I have never yet seen anybody with real power who did not first have inner quietness. The person who is torn apart inside has no focus, no strength, no vigor. To have energy and force and to be able to direct it, you have to have peace at the center. The inwardly quiet man is the strong, effective man.

Whatever the circumstances of your life, put your trust in Jesus. He has the keys to the Kingdom of Heaven. He can guide you through the problems and the sorrows and the difficulties of this life. That inner peace you have always wanted can be found by finding Him. You find Him by simply saying, "Lord, I'll fight this battle with myself. I'll let myself go. I give myself to You. I'll do the thing You want me to do. I won't compromise. I'll follow Your way." It isn't an easy way, but it brings that great, priceless thing—the inner peace you've always wanted. If you want it badly enough, you can have it, through Him.